Published in the UK in 2026 by Post Wave Children's Books,
an imprint of Post Wave Publishing UK Ltd,
Runway East, 24-28 Bloomsbury Way, London, WC1A 2SN
www.postwavepublishing.com

A catalogue record of this book is available from the British Library.

First edition 2025, published with permission of Éditions La Doux

First published in France under the title: *Merveilleux Caca*

English translation rights arranged through Ttipi agency, France

1 3 5 7 9 10 8 6 4 2
0426 002

ISBN 978-1-83627-2-236

Printed and manufactured in China by Leo Paper Products, Heshan, Guangdong, April 2026.

This book conforms to General Product Safety Regulation (GPSR) requirements.
EU authorised representative: Harriet Birkinshaw, Post Wave Berlin Studio
Email: GPSR@postwavepublishing.com
Address: Post Wave Berlin Studio, c/o Mindspace, Skalitzer Straße 104, 10997 Berlin, Germany

FSC www.fsc.org MIX Paper | Supporting responsible forestry FSC® C020056

MARVELLOUS POO

MATHIS

post wave

WHAT IS POO?

Poo is what's left of the food you have eaten and what your body hasn't used. It is the result of an incredible transformation that takes place inside your body. This transformation is called **DIGESTION**.

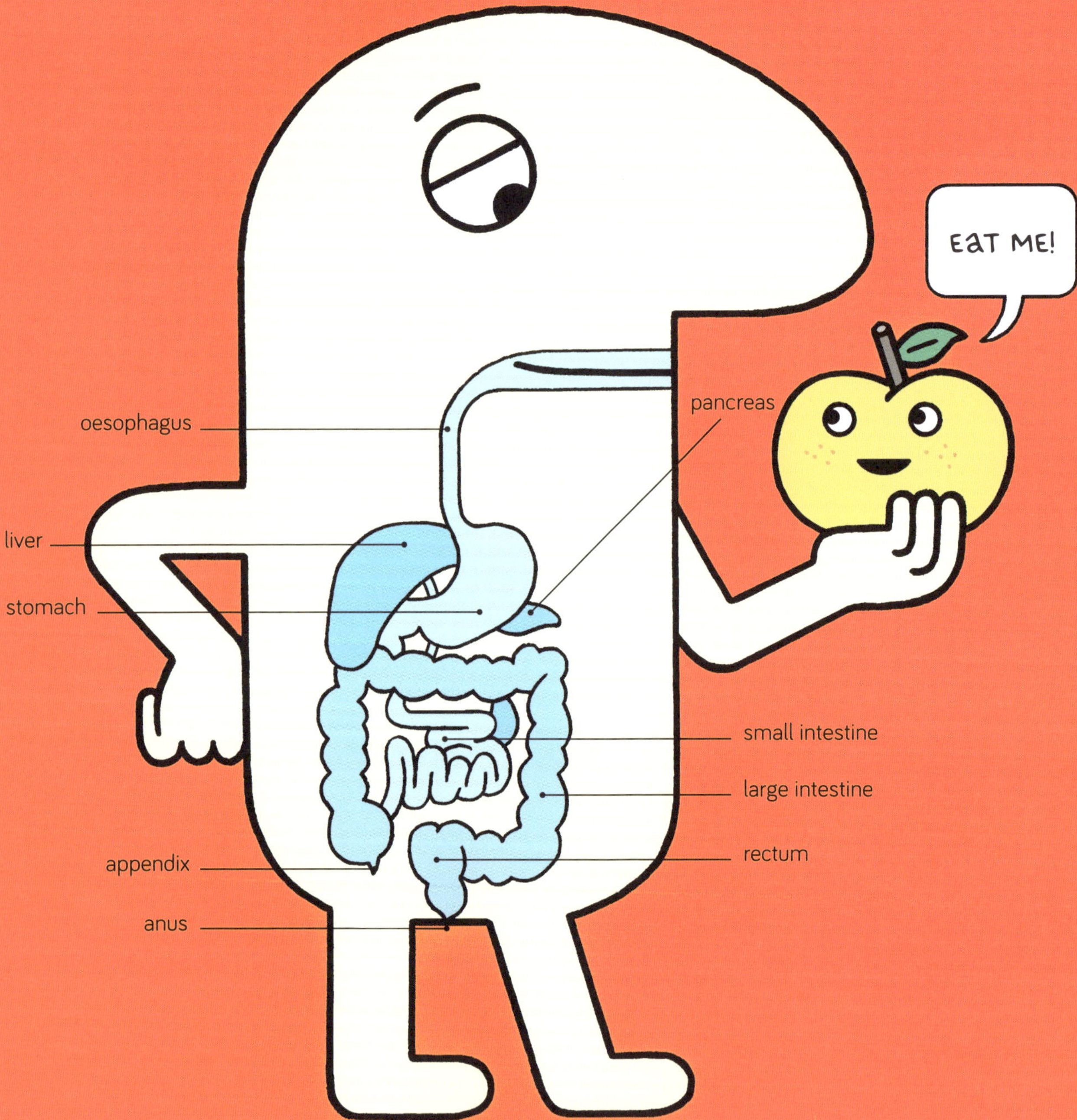

DIGESTION

1 Digestion begins when you start chewing your food. Your saliva mixes with it to help break it down.

2 The chewed food moves down the body, through the oesophagus and then into the stomach.

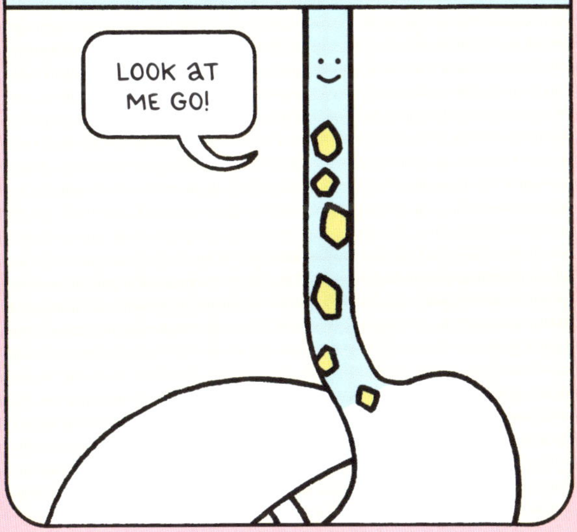

3 In the stomach, the food is mixed and broken down into even smaller pieces.

4 The liver and pancreas help digestion by producing chemicals.

5 In the small intestine, the nutrients from food pass into the blood to feed the body.

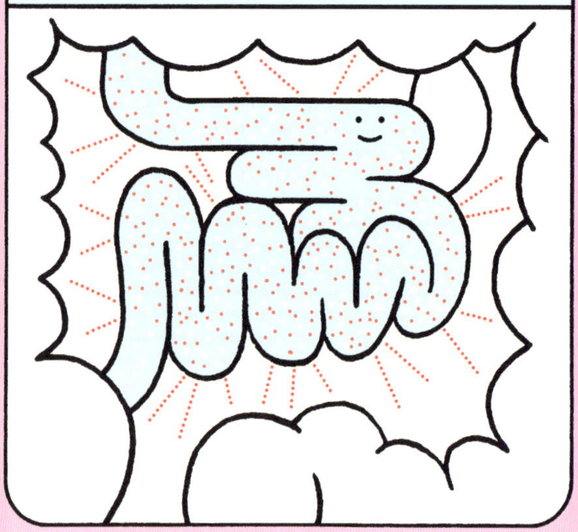

6 In the large intestine, what's left of the food turns into poo – waste that your body doesn't need anymore.

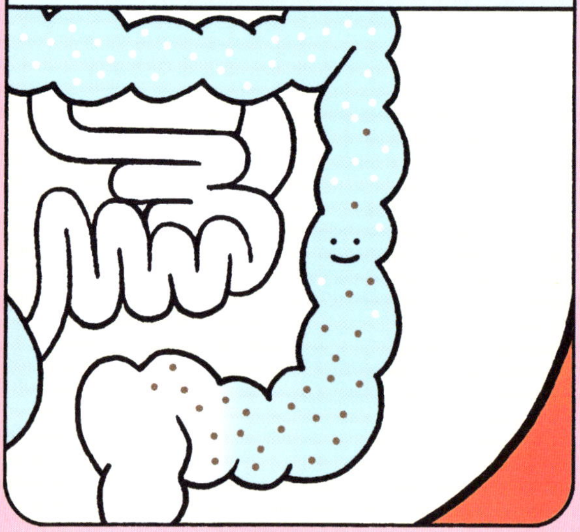

7 The rectum is at the end of the intestine. This is where poo waits before coming out.

8 The anus is a muscle that holds poo in and lets it out when you go to the toilet.

WHERE DO WE POO?

In a nappy

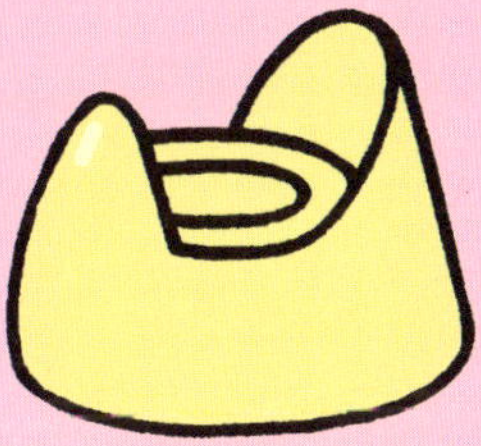
In a potty

In a toilet

In a composting toilet

In a boat toilet

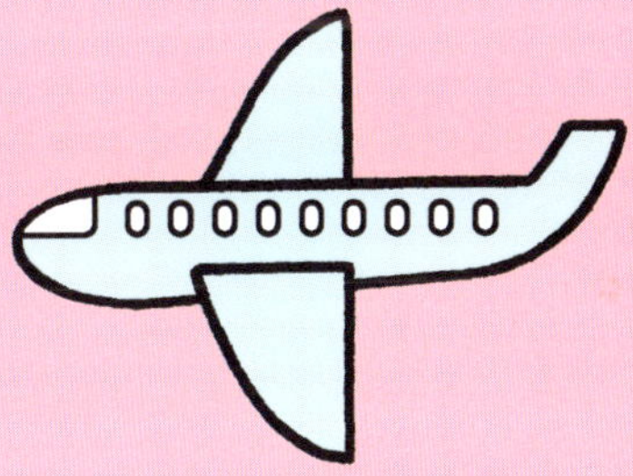
In a plane toilet

In a coach toilet

In a train toilet

In nature

POO SHAPES
(AND WHAT THEY MEAN)

hazelnuts

bumpy sausage

cracked sausage

soft grapes

the foamy one

the runny one

sticky sausage (sticks to the bowl)

perfect sausage!

POO COLOURS

HELLO, I'M A BROWN POO. I'M TOTALLY NORMAL!
HELLO, I'M GREEN. I'M BABY POO!
OR MAYBE YOU'VE EATEN LOTS OF GREEN FOOD!
OH DEAR, I'M YELLOW, YOU'RE EATING TOO MUCH FAT!
I'M A BLACK POO. THERE'S TOO MUCH IRON IN YOUR BLOOD! GO SEE A DOCTOR.
I'M COLOURLESS – YOU'D BETTER SEE A DOCTOR.
HI, I'M RED. MAYBE YOU ATE A LOT OF RED FOOD. IF NOT, GO SEE A DOCTOR!
OOH, YOU'VE EATEN TOO MANY PEAS!
CAREFUL! YOU'RE EATING TOO MANY SWEETS!
MY FRIENDS ON MY LEFT ARE JOKERS! WE'RE REALLY THREE DELICIOUS LITTLE MERINGUES!

WHO POOS?

Babies poo

Children poo

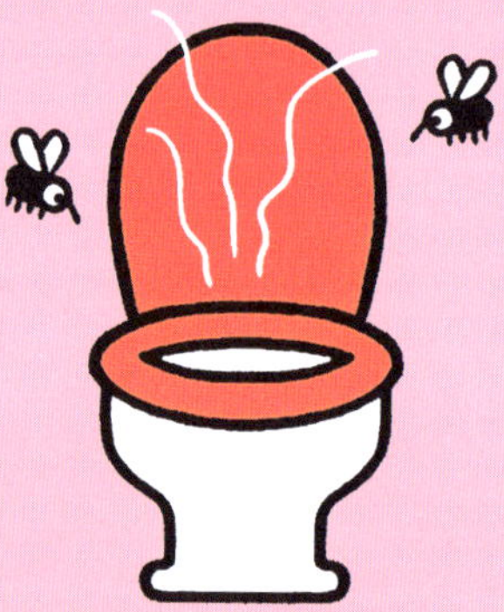

Mums and dads poo

Teachers poo

Kings and queens poo

Doctors poo

Singers poo

Santa poos

Clowns poo

EVERYONE POOS!

WHERE DOES MY POO GO?

When you flush the toilet, your poo begins an incredible journey . . .

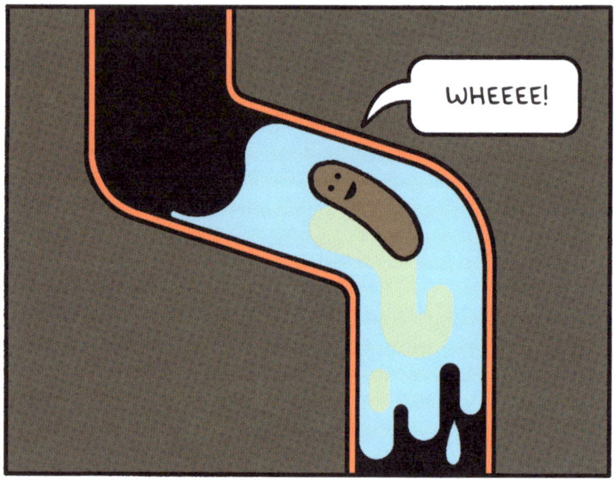

Your poo gets a ride on a superfast log flume!

Splash! Your poo and wee arrive in the sewers (big underground pipes that carry dirty water away from toilets, showers, bathtubs and sinks).

In the sewers, your poo bumps into other poos.

The poos bob along happily until they reach . . .

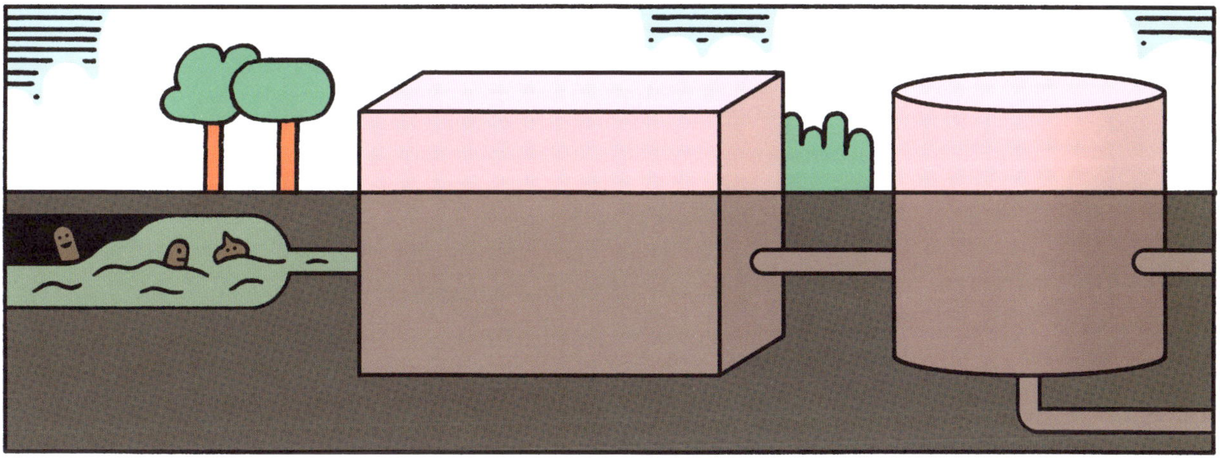

. . . the wastewater treatment plant!

Here, they are mixed up and passed through filters
(grids that get finer and finer).

The poos, now turned into sludge,
are stored in a big tank.

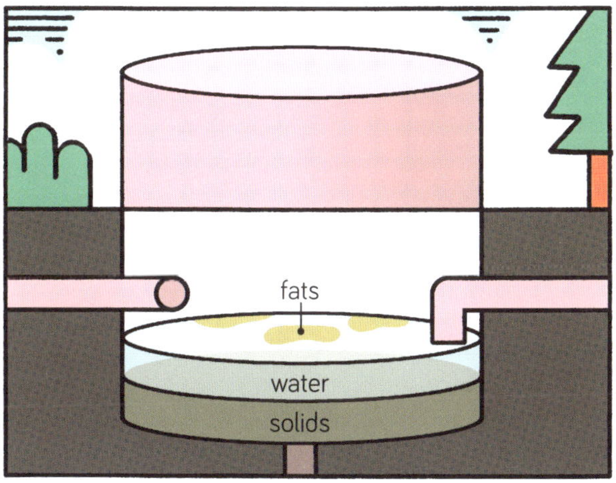

Over time, the solid parts sink
to the bottom of the tank.

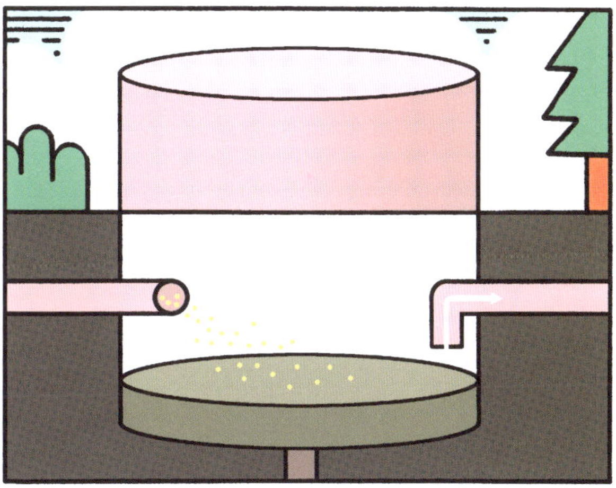

The fats and water are sucked away.
The solid part is disinfected (made clean).

The solid matter is then taken out of the tank and turned into pellets.

The pellets are packed into bags.

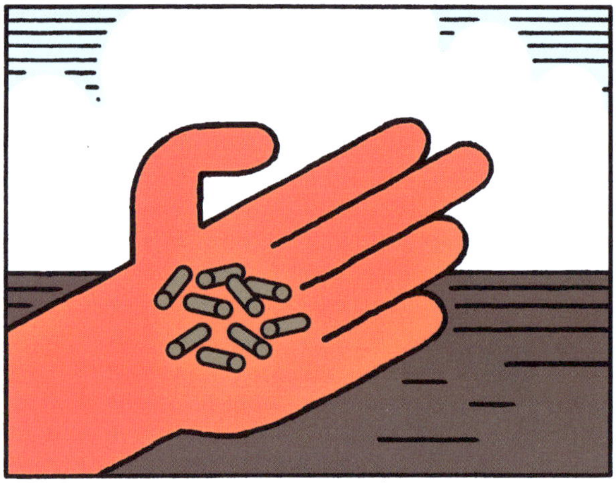

They are full of nutrients (chemicals that help things grow and be healthy).

The pellets are mixed with soil.

Once in the soil, they feed the plants. Plants need food to grow, just like humans!

When the sun shines and the rain pours . . .

. . . the plants become big and strong!

SO, WHO LOVES POO?

ALL PLANTS, TREES, FLOWERS AND FUNGI LOVE POO!

ANIMALS AND POO

Many insects, like beetles, feed on dung.
The most well-known animals that eat poo are:

flies

dung beetles

earthworms

Poo contains food for insects and plants. When insects break poo down into small, bitesize pieces, it increases soil fertility and helps plants grow.

The dung beetle stores its food by burying balls of dung. Plants benefit from this because their roots can reach nutrients left by the poo!

RABBITS EAT THEIR POO!

Some animals, like hares and rabbits, digest their food too quickly. Hard droppings mean their digestive system is working well, but their soft droppings contain many nutrients that shouldn't be wasted. This is why they eat their poo!

OTHER ANIMALS THAT EAT THEIR OWN POO

gorilla

beaver

koala

shrew

rat

parrot

AMAZING POOS

The wombat is a marsupial that lives in Australia. As an adult, it weighs between 20 and 35 kilograms. It is the only animal to produce cube-shaped droppings. This is due to the different thicknesses of the muscles in its intestine.

Whale poo is pinkish orange because it eats a lot of krill (a type of tiny shrimp). A whale produces about 40 kilograms of poo per day – that's about the size of a labrador!

The Goliath beetle, one of the world's largest insects, produces the largest amount of poo relative to its weight. Once, a Goliath beetle weighing 22 grams, weighed only 14 grams after pooing! It lost almost half its weight!

THE WORLD CHAMPION POOPER

Elephants poo between 12 and 15 times a day!

They produce 100 kilograms of dung daily.

In Japan, beer is made from elephant poo.

Elephant dung contains a lot of fibre. In Sri Lanka and Thailand, it is used to make paper.

In Thailand, bricks are made with water, cement and elephant poo.

18 to 19 centimetres

Elephant droppings are a little smaller than a football.

POO FACTS

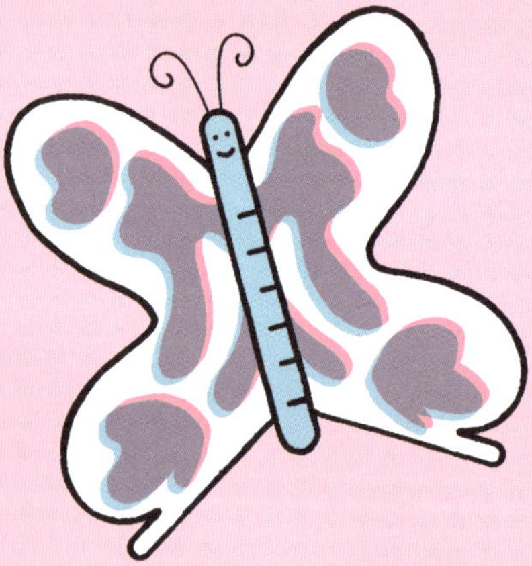

Butterflies don't poo because their food is liquid. They only pee! But when they are caterpillars they poo a lot.

The bacteria that break down our food in the intestine are responsible for the smell of poo.

Termites use their excrement as a material to build their nests.

Like us, ants have a special place in their homes to do their business.

THE MANY NAMES FOR POO

LET'S TALK POO

SOME WAYS TO SAY: I'M GOING TO POOP!

THE FOUR LITTLE POOS

(And now it's time for a poo-tiful story!)

One fresh poo is walking in the forest.
Who goes there?
Who are you?
Why, it's another little poo!
Yoohoo!

Two fresh poos are walking in the forest.
Look – over there!
Who are you?
Why, it's another little poo!
Yoohoo!

Three not-so-fresh poos come out of the forest.
Hello! Who are you?
Hello, my name is Poo!
Yoohoo!

Four tired poos have settled in the grass.
Who's that? Oh my! It's a poo eater!
RUUUUUUUUN!